Making Toys
That Crawl
and Slide

Making Toys
That Crawl and Slide

Alice Gilbreath

**illustrated by
Joe Rogers**

Follett Publishing Company
Chicago

International Standard Book Number: 0-695-40961-1
Titan binding
International Standard Book Number: 0-695-30961-7
Paper binding

Second Printing

To Shelly Green

Crawling Caterpillar

To make a caterpillar, you will need these things:

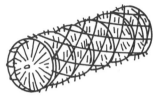

brush hair roller

two roller pins

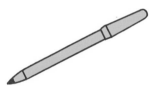

felt marker

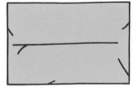

piece of tissue bigger than your hand

When you have all these things, follow these steps:

1.   The hair roller is the caterpillar's body. The pins are the caterpillar's feelers. Put the pins in the hair roller. Put them at one end of the roller. Put them about two fingers apart.

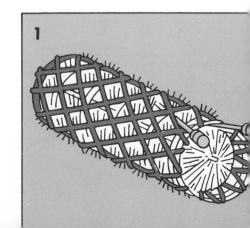

2. Roll the tissue into a ball. Make the ball as big as the end of the roller. The tissue ball is the caterpillar's head.

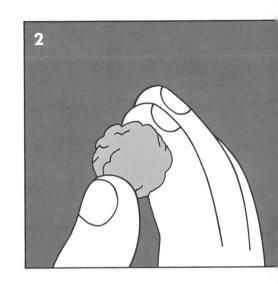

3. Put the tissue ball in the roller body. Put it in the same end as the caterpillar's feelers.

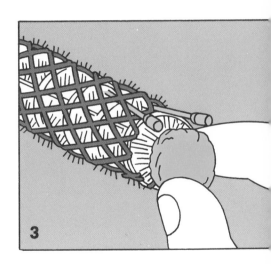

4. With the felt marker, draw on the tissue. Draw the caterpillar's face. Your caterpillar is finished. Move it with your fingers.

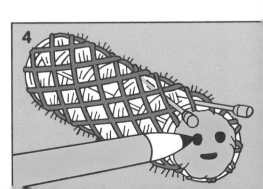

Toboggan and Rider

To make a toboggan and rider, you will need these things:

piece of thin, corrugated cardboard (such as one side of a light bulb box)

colored paper

glue

paint

paintbrush

felt marker

scissors

When you have all these things, follow these steps:

1. With your marker, draw a rectangle on the cardboard. Draw it as wide as your hand. Draw it as long as two hands.

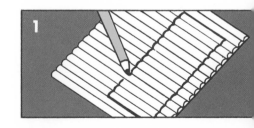

2. With your scissors, cut out the rectangle.

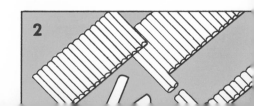

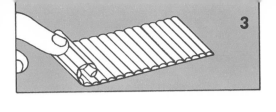

3. The cardboard rectangle is the toboggan. With your fingers, roll one end of the toboggan. Roll it tightly about two times around.

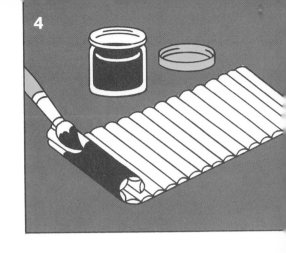

4. With your paintbrush, paint the little roll. Let the paint dry. The little roll is the front of the toboggan.

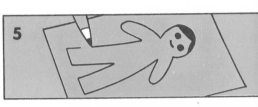

5. With your felt marker, draw on the colored paper. Draw a boy or girl.

6. With your scissors, cut out the boy or girl.

7. With your fingers, bend the boy or girl in the middle.

8. Put a line of glue on the toboggan. Put the boy or girl on the glue. Let the glue dry. Your toboggan and rider are finished.

Tiny Turtle

To make a turtle, you will need these things:

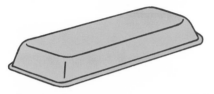

plastic foam egg carton lid

felt marker

plastic foam egg carton cup

half a pipe cleaner

scissors

When you have all these things, follow these steps:

1. The egg cup is the turtle's shell. With your felt marker, draw on the shell. Draw the turtle's feet. Draw marks all over the turtle's shell.

2. With your fingers, push the pipe cleaner through the turtle's shell. Push it in one side of the shell. Push it out the other side of the shell.

3. One end of the pipe cleaner is the turtle's tail. The other end of the pipe cleaner is the turtle's neck. With your fingers, bend the turtle's neck up.

4. With your felt marker, draw a circle on the egg carton lid. Make the circle as big as a quarter. The circle is the turtle's head. Draw a face on it. With your scissors, cut out the turtle's face.

5. With your fingers, put the turtle's face on the turtle's neck. Push the pipe cleaner through the middle of the circle. Your turtle is finished. Make it move with your fingers.

Crane

To make a crane, you will need these things:

small Jell-O box with the end taped shut

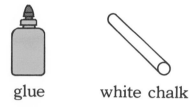

glue   white chalk

piece of string longer than your hand

small raisin box with the flap closed

paint   paintbrush

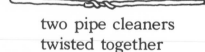

two pipe cleaners twisted together

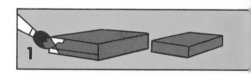

small magnet with sticky ba (from a hobby or craft shop)

When you have all these things, follow these steps:

1. With your paintbrush, paint the boxes. Let the paint dry.

2. With the chalk, draw marks on the bigger box. The marks are the crane's treads.

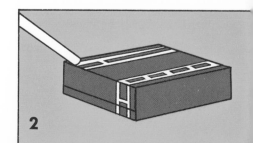

3. With your fingers, tie the string. Tie it to the pipe cleaners. Tie it to the place where the pipe cleaners are twisted together.

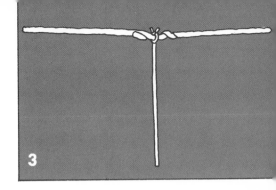

4. With your fingers, peel the backing off the magnet. Put the magnet on the string. Put the sticky side on the end of the string.

5. Bend the pipe cleaners at the twist. Put both ends of the pipe cleaners in the box.

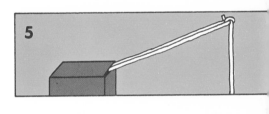

6. Put glue on the small box. Put it on one end of the box.

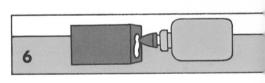

7. Put the small box on the bigger box. Put it in the center of the bigger box. Let the glue dry. Your crane is finished. It will pick up paper clips or small nails.

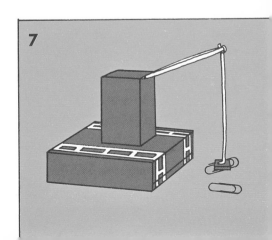

Snail

To make a snail, you will need these things:

small magnet with sticky back (from a hobby or craft shop)

larger magnet

piece of cardboard

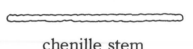

chenille stem

When you have all these things, follow these steps:

1. With your fingers, bend the chenille stem. Bend it as far as one finger. Bend it back. This is the snail's foot. The snail's foot is at the bottom of the snail.

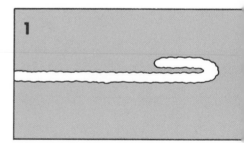

2. With your fingers, bend the chenille stem. Bend the other end of the stem. Bend it into a circle. Bend it around and around. This is the snail's shell.

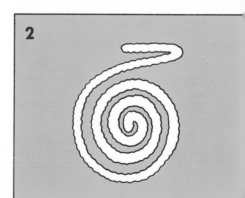

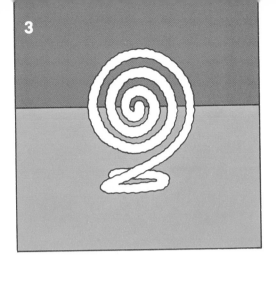

3. Bend the snail's shell. Bend it above the snail's foot.

4. With your fingers, peel the backing off the small magnet. Put the snail on the magnet. Put the snail's foot on the sticky side of the magnet.

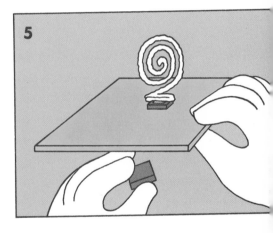

5. Put your snail on the cardboard. Put the larger magnet under the cardboard. Put it under the snail.

6. With your fingers, move the larger magnet. The snail will move, too.

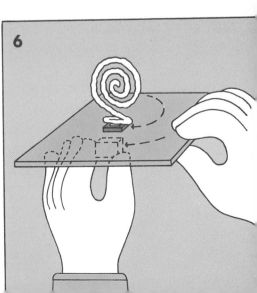

Baby

To make the baby, you will need these things:

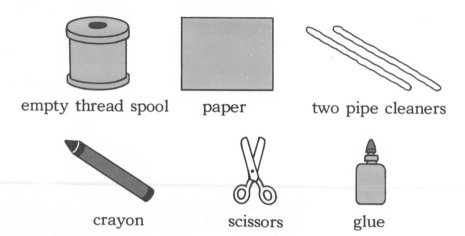

empty thread spool   paper   two pipe cleaners

crayon   scissors   glue

When you have all these things, follow these steps:

1. With your fingers, twist the pipe cleaners. Twist the middle of one pipe cleaner around the middle of the other pipe cleaner. Twist it around three times.

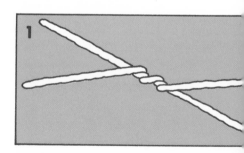

2. Put the pipe cleaners through the spool. The pipe cleaners are the baby's arms and legs. The spool is the baby's body.

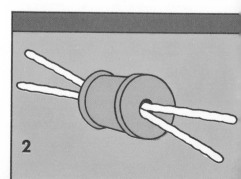

16

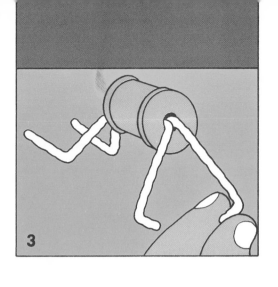

3. With your fingers, bend the baby's arms down. Bend the hands. Bend the baby's legs down. Bend the knees.

4. With your crayon, draw a circle on the paper. Draw the baby's face in the circle.

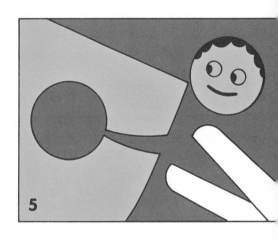

5. With your scissors, cut out the face.

6. Put glue on the baby's body. Put it above the baby's arms. Put the baby's face on the glue. Let the glue dry. The baby is finished.

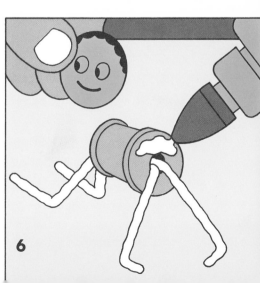

Inchworm

To make an inchworm, you will need these things:

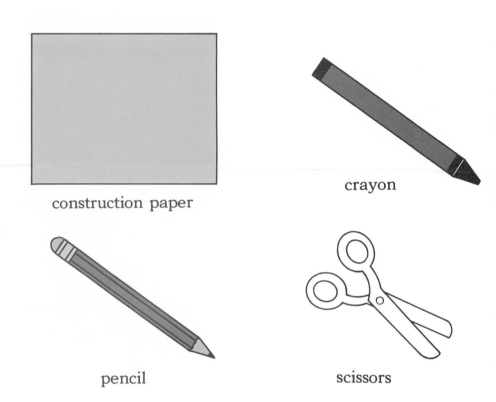

construction paper

crayon

pencil

scissors

When you have all these things, follow these steps:

1. With your pencil, draw an inchworm. Draw it as long as two hands. Draw it as wide as two fingers.

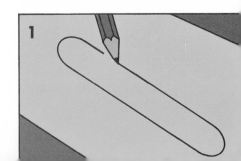

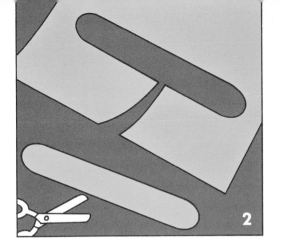

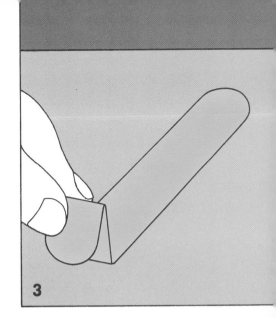

2. With your scissors, cut out the inchworm.

3. With your fingers, bend the inchworm. Bend down a piece as wide as two fingers. Bend the inchworm up.

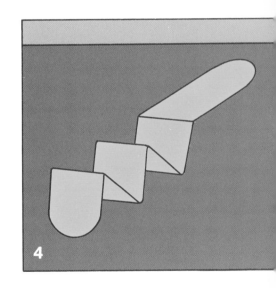

4. Bend down another piece. Bend the inchworm up again. Keep bending down, then up, across the whole inchworm.

5. With your crayon, draw a face on the inchworm. Your inchworm is finished. Move it with your fingers to make it crawl.

Skier

To make a skier, you will need these things:

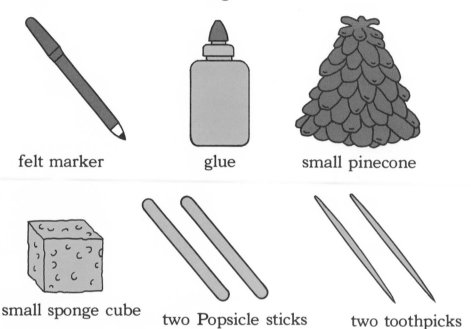

felt marker   glue   small pinecone

small sponge cube   two Popsicle sticks   two toothpicks

 twister with wire inside

When you have all these things, follow these steps:

1. The twister is the skier's arms. The toothpicks are the ski poles. Put a ski pole in each of the skier's arms. Bend the hands around the ski poles.

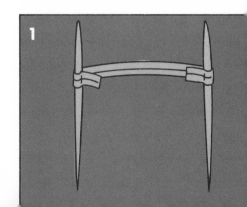

2. The pinecone is the skier's body. Bend the arms with the ski poles around the skier's body.

3. The sponge is the skier's head. With the felt marker, draw a face on the skier's head. Draw hair on the skier's head.

4. Put glue on the bottom of the skier's head. Put the skier's head on the skier's body. Let the glue dry.

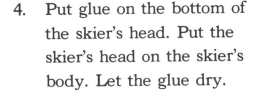

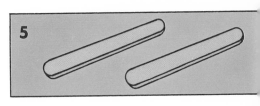

5. The Popsicle sticks are the skis. Put the skis on a table.

6. Put glue on each ski. Put the skier on the glue. Let the glue dry. Your skier is finished.

Centipede

To make a centipede, you will
need these things:

piece of thin rope or heavy
cord as long as your hand

string

paper   crayon   glue   scissors

When you have all these things, follow these steps:

1. With your scissors, cut the
   string. Cut twelve pieces.
   Cut each one as long as
   one finger. The pieces of
   string are the centipede's
   legs.

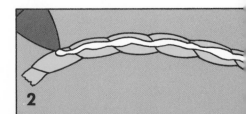

2. The rope is the centipede's
   body. Put glue on the
   centipede's body.

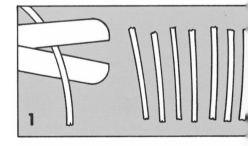

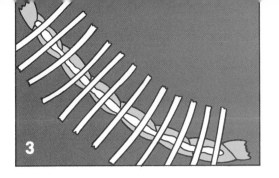

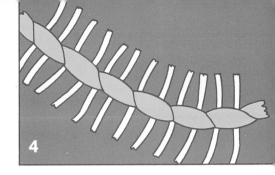

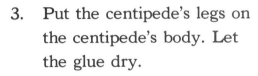

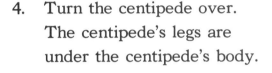

3. Put the centipede's legs on the centipede's body. Let the glue dry.

4. Turn the centipede over. The centipede's legs are under the centipede's body.

5. With your crayon, draw a circle. Draw it on the paper. Make it as big as a dime. Draw a face in the circle.

6. With your scissors, cut out the centipede's face.

7. Put glue on the end of the centipede's body. Put the centipede's face on the glue. Let the glue dry. Your centipede is finished. Move it with your fingers.

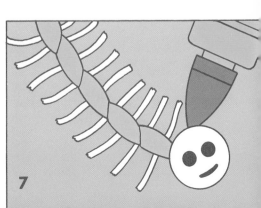

 # Sleigh

To make a sleigh, you will need these things:

construction paper

small cereal box with the back cut out

paint

paintbrush

pencil

scissors

When you have all these things, follow these steps:

1. With your paintbrush, paint the box. Paint the inside of the box. Paint the outside of the box. Let the paint dry. The box is the sleigh box.

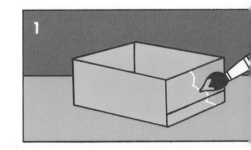

2. With your fingers, fold the paper. Fold it in the center.

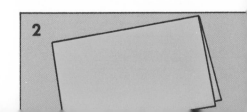

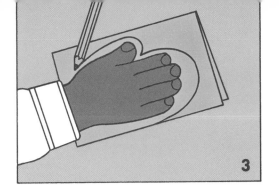

3. Put one hand on the folded paper. With a pencil, draw a mitten. Draw it around your hand.

4. With your scissors, cut out the mitten. Cut both pieces of paper. Now you have two mittens.

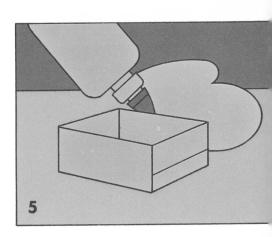

5. Put glue on the box. Put it on one side of the box. Put one mitten on the glue. Let the glue dry.

6. Put glue on the other side of the box. Put the second mitten on the glue. Let the glue dry. The mittens are the sides of the sleigh. Your sleigh is finished. Let toys ride in it.

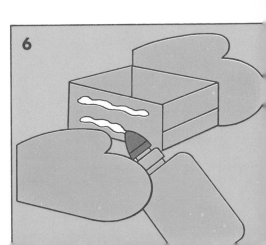

Snowmobile

To make a snowmobile, you will need these things:

pencil   scissors

half an egg carton

egg carton lid   paint   paintbrush   glue

When you have all these things, follow these steps:

1. With your pencil, draw on the egg carton half. Draw a line across the lid. Draw the line two egg cups from the end. Make the line go up one side of the lid, across the top, and down the other side.

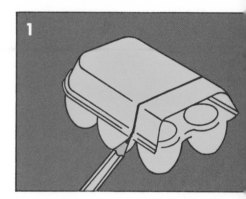

2. Draw another line on the egg carton. Draw it along the fold where the lid joins the egg cups. Make the line one egg cup long.

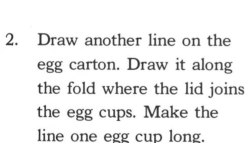

3. Open up the egg carton. With your scissors, cut off one piece of lid. Cut along the lines you drew.

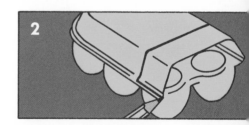

4. Close the egg carton. The egg carton is the body of the snowmobile.

5. With your paintbrush, paint the snowmobile. Paint headlights. Paint the top.

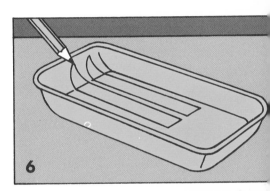

6. With your pencil, draw on the other egg carton lid. Draw two snowmobile runners. Draw them as long as two hands. Draw them as wide as two fingers. Draw up one end of the lid. Draw the tips of the runners.

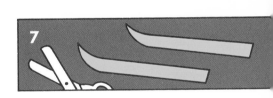

7. With your scissors, cut out the runners.

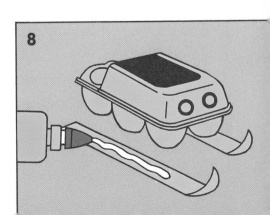

8. Put a line of glue on each runner. Put the snowmobile on the glue. Let the glue dry. Your snowmobile is finished. Let toys ride in the seats.

Spider

To make a spider, you will need these things:

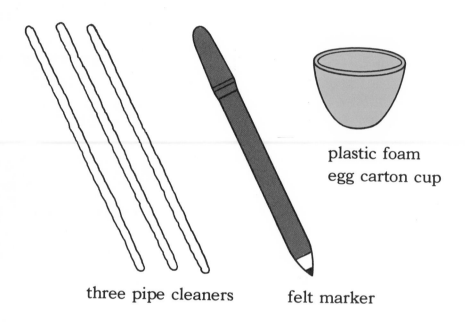

three pipe cleaners

felt marker

plastic foam egg carton cup

When you have all these things, follow these steps:

1. With your fingers, put one pipe cleaner in the egg cup. Put it near the front of the egg cup. Push it in one side. Push it out the other side.

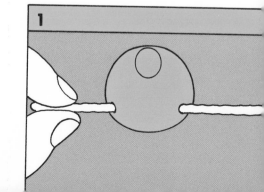

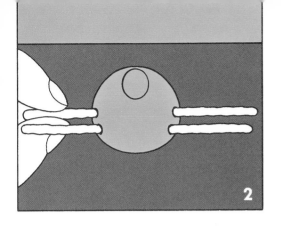
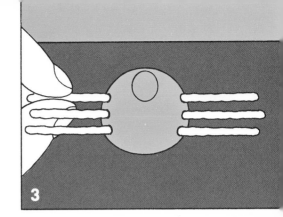

2. Put another pipe cleaner in the egg cup. Put it near the center of the egg cup. Push it in one side. Push it out the other side.

3. Put the last pipe cleaner in the egg cup the same way. Put it near the back of the egg cup.

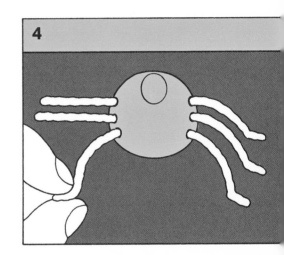

4. The egg cup is the spider's body. The pipe cleaners are the spider's legs. Bend the spider's legs. Bend the ends of the legs.

5. With your felt marker, draw the spider's face. Your spider is finished. Move it with your fingers.

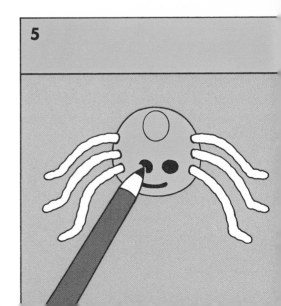

Crocodile

To make a crocodile, you will need these things:

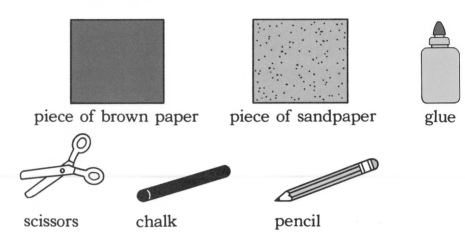

piece of brown paper   piece of sandpaper   glue

scissors   chalk   pencil

When you have all these things, follow these steps:

1. With your fingers, fold the sandpaper. Fold it in the center. The fold is the crocodile's backbone. Open the sandpaper.

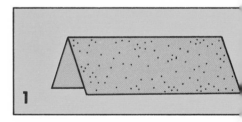

2. With your pencil, draw a big crocodile. Draw it as long as the sandpaper. Draw a big mouth. Draw four short legs. Draw a big tail.

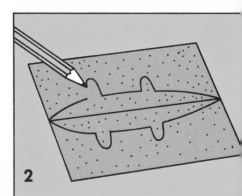

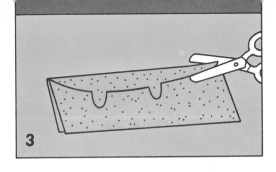

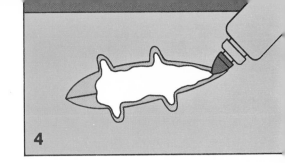

3. With your scissors, cut out the crocodile.

4. Put glue on the crocodile. Put it on the underside of the crocodile. Put it on the crocodile's body but not the crocodile's mouth.

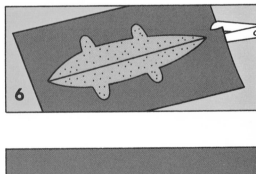

5. Put the crocodile on the paper. Let the glue dry.

6. With your scissors, cut out the crocodile.

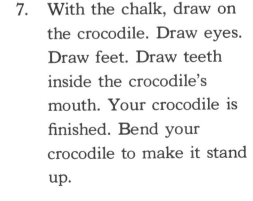

7. With the chalk, draw on the crocodile. Draw eyes. Draw feet. Draw teeth inside the crocodile's mouth. Your crocodile is finished. Bend your crocodile to make it stand up.

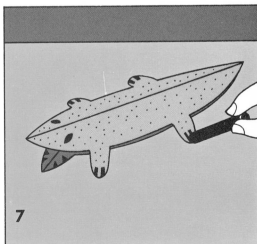

Creepy Crawler

To make a creepy crawler, you will need these things:

scissors

felt marker

hair clip

four rubber bands

When you have all these things, follow these steps:

1. With the felt marker, draw a face on the creepy crawler. Draw spots on the creepy crawler's body.

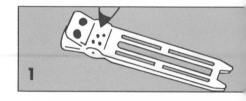

2. With your fingers, open the creepy crawler's body. Put the rubber bands in the body. Close the body.

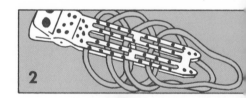

3. Cut three rubber bands. Slide them to the back of the creepy crawler. These are the legs. Slide the last rubber band to the front of the creepy crawler. Do not cut it. Pull your creepy crawler with the front rubber band.

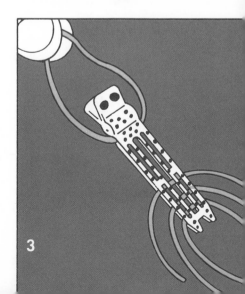